MAHABHARATA STORIES

The Ashram of Dronacharya

Subhadra Sen Gupta

Om Books International

When the Pandavas returned to Hastinapur, the eldest–Yudhishthira–was sixteen years old. Bhishma and the chief minister, Vidura, welcomed them and they began to live in the palace. The sons of Dhritarashtra and Gandhari were called the Kauravas. The sons of Pandu, Kunti and Madri were the Pandavas.

The Pandavas combined all the traits of a king–honesty, strength, skill, beauty and wisdom–and were blessed with the qualities of their fathers. Yudhishthira as the son of Dharma was a scholar, who always spoke the truth and believed in justice.

Arjuna was the son of Indra, the Commander-in-Chief of the Gods. He was the best archer among all the princes and a brave fighter.

Bhima was the son of Vayu, the Wind God, and he was the strongest among them all. No one could defeat him in wrestling. The twins, Nakul and Sahadev, were the sons of the Ashwins. Nakul had a pleasing personality and Sahadev was a wise man who could see the future. Bhishma said to Vidura, "The Pandavas may have grown up in the forest but they are princes. They should be educated and trained as warriors."

Vidura said, "I agree. Also, as the eldest of the cousins, Yudhishthira will one day become king and he has to have all the qualities of a king." He asked, "Who can teach the boys? We need a great guru."

Duryodhana, Shakuni and Dhritarashtra met in secret. Duryodhana said to Shakuni, "We have to get rid of the Pandavas. You are a clever man, think of a plan."

Shakuni gave a crafty smile, "It will be done, Duryodhana!"

At the same time, Dhritarashtra was very unhappy as he knew that Duryodhana would not become the next king. Yudhishthira would sit on the throne next because he was the eldest grandson of Vichitravirya and he was loved by the people of Hastinapur for his kindness and sense of justice.

Duryodhana called his uncle Shakuni and said, "We Kauravas always lose to the Pandavas when it comes to fighting. This is making me very angry."

Shakuni laughed, "And one day when Yudhishthira becomes king, he, Bhima and Arjuna will throw the Kauravas out of the kingdom."

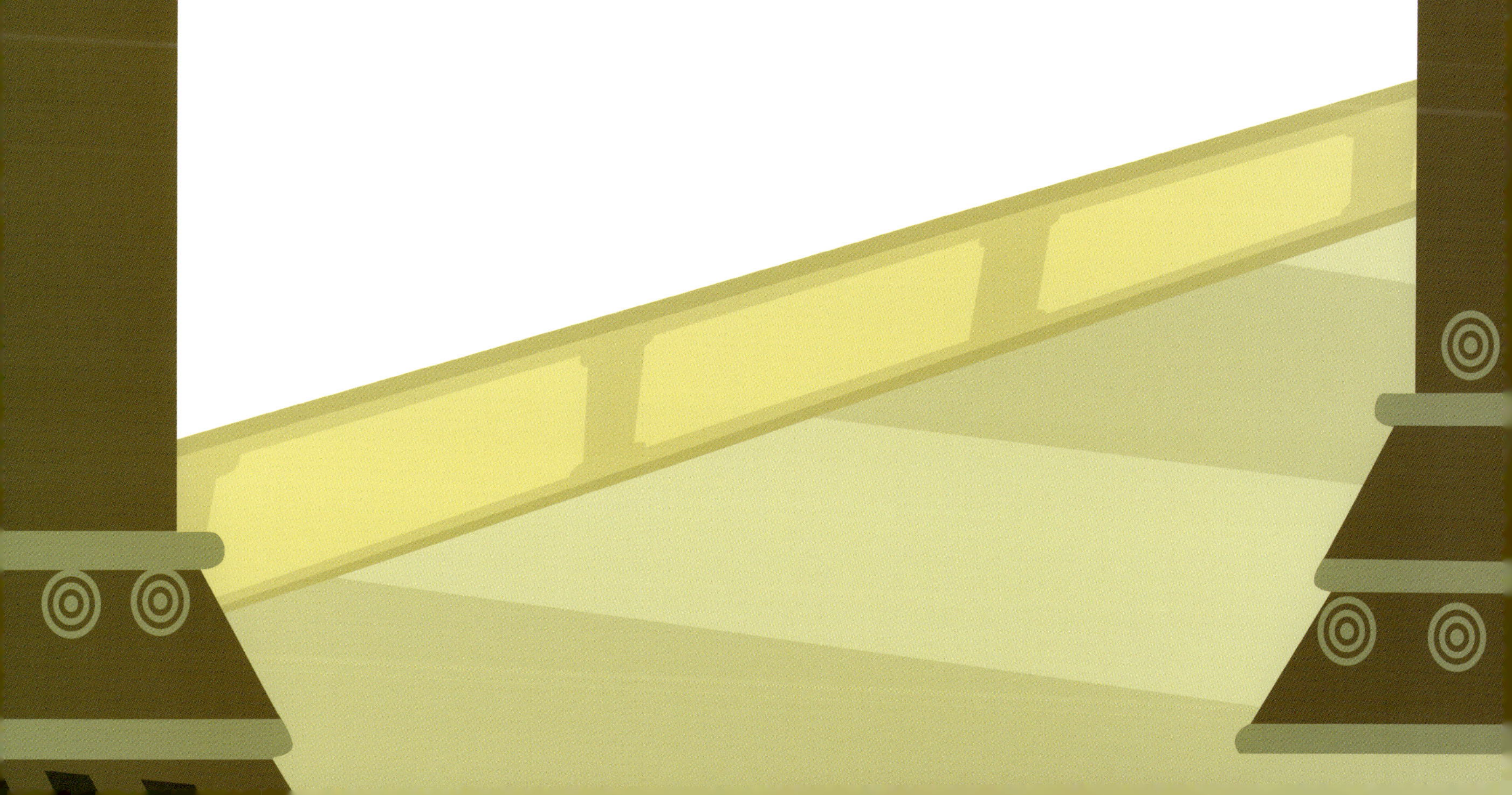

The two strongest boys were the second Pandava, Bhima and the eldest Kaurava, Duryodhana. When they fought with the mace or challenged each other to a wrestling match, it was a mighty battle. What made Duryodhana angry was that even though he fought very hard, he was always defeated by Bhima.

The Kauravas were full of envy at the fighting skills of the Pandavas. When it came to using the bow and arrow, no one could defeat Arjuna. He could aim for the eye of a toy bird placed among the branches of a tree and pierce it with just one arrow.

Dronacharya taught the Pandavas and Kauravas all the skills of warriors, so that they could defeat the enemy in the battlefield. They learnt to ride horses and drive chariots. They were taught to fight with swords and shields, spears, maces and battle-axes.

Guru Dronacharya said to the boys, "You are the sons of kings, and as the princes of the great kingdom of Hastinapur, you have to become scholars by reading the sacred books. Also you have to learn the art of fighting a battle and become warriors."

Bhishma said, "Summon Guru Dronacharya. He is the finest teacher in the kingdom. He will teach the Pandavas and Kauravas to become great warriors."

The Pandavas and Kauravas were sent to the ashram of Guru Dronacharya. The ashram was in a forest and they had to live in huts and study the sacred books. And, Guru Kripacharya taught them archery.